# THANKSGIVING

## HOLIDAYS

Lynda Sorensen

The Rourke Press, Inc.
Vero Beach, Florida 32964

Edited by Sandra A. Robinson

PHOTO CREDITS
© Plimoth Plantation: pages 7, 8, 10, 12-13, 21; © Lynn M. Stone:
cover, title page, pages 4, 17, 18; © James P. Rowan: page 15

**Library of Congress Cataloging-in-Publication Data**

Sorensen, Lynda, 1953-
    Thanksgiving / Lynda Sorensen.
    p.  cm. — (Holidays)
    ISBN 1-57103-072-7
    1. Thanksgiving Day—Juvenile literature. 2. United States—
Social life and customs—Juvenile literature. [1. Thanksgiving Day.]
I. Title. II. Series: Sorensen, Lynda, 1953-  Holidays.
GT4975.S67  1994
394.2'649—dc20
                        94-17723
                        CIP
                        AC

Printed in the USA

# TABLE OF CONTENTS

# THANKSGIVING

On Thanksgiving Day, people remember their blessings and give thanks for them. Many people attend Thanksgiving church services. Families gather together to share Thanksgiving meals and enjoy family **traditions,** or customs.

The fourth Thursday in November is Thanksgiving Day. It is a **national** holiday in the United States. Canada celebrates Thanksgiving on the second Monday in October.

*Thanksgiving Day celebrates the harvest and blessings of the year*

# THE PILGRIMS

After crossing the Atlantic Ocean aboard the ship *Mayflower,* the Pilgrims arrived on the shore of what is now Massachusetts in December, 1620. Facing great hardships, they founded a village, Plimoth Colony.

The first winter was very cold and food was scarce. Disease killed one-half of the **colonists.**

The colonists who survived were determined to stay in this "New World." With the help of Squanto and other friendly Native Americans, the colonists planted crops in the spring.

*The know-how of friendly Native Americans, such as Squanto, helped some of the Pilgrims survive a harsh winter*

## A FIRST THANKSGIVING

With a good harvest in the fall of 1621, the colonists found new hope and plentiful food. William Bradford, governor of the colony, set aside time for **recreation** and thanks to God for the harvest.

The Pilgrims' letters and diaries tell that they invited their Native American neighbors to join them in three days of fun and feasting. They ran races and played games. They ate deer, ducks, geese, swans, wild turkeys, corn meal, fish and fruit.

*The Fall Harvest Feast at Plimoth Colony in 1621 was three days of fun and food*

# EARLY THANKSGIVINGS

The colonists didn't mention celebrating the harvest of 1622. Perhaps crops were poor. From time to time, however, the Pilgrims held days of thanksgiving for special reasons.

These were holy days for prayer and church. The days included meals, but not fun and games.

*The harsh New England winters killed many of the Pilgrims*

*The Pilgrims' days of thanksgiving were*

*serious events, not at all like the Harvest Festival*

## THE FIRST NATIONAL THANKSGIVING

The Continental Congress declared the first national Thanksgiving in 1777. The Continental Congress was a group of **delegates** from the 13 English colonies in America.

The country had grown quickly after the Pilgrims' arrival. In 1777, the colonists were fighting a war against England. They wanted to be free and independent of English rule.

That first nationwide Thanksgiving, like the old Pilgrim days of thanksgiving, was a quiet, serious celebration. It was a day of prayer and rest from regular work.

*Soldiers from the American colonies were battling the English in 1777 when the Continental Congress declared the first national Thanksgiving*

# THANKSGIVING IN THE NEW NATION

The colonies defeated England in the Revolutionary War (1776-1783). They won their freedom and the United States of America was born. George Washington, the nation's first president, called for a nationwide day of Thanksgiving. President Washington wanted Americans to thank God for victory in the war.

A Thanksgiving tradition had begun in America, but it did not last. By 1816, Thanksgiving had almost disappeared!

*Thanks for plentiful food has been a part of modern Thanksgivings in America*

## SARAH HALE'S CAMPAIGN

Mrs. Sarah J. Hale helped bring Thanksgiving back. Mrs. Hale, who wrote "Mary Had a Little Lamb," was a well-known writer and editor. In 1827 she began an effort to make Thanksgiving a national holiday. Many years later, President Abraham Lincoln made her effort a success. In 1863 Mr. Lincoln ordered that *two* Thanksgivings be held.

Each president after Lincoln continued to celebrate a Thanksgiving Day in November. In 1941 the United States **Congress** made Thanksgiving a national holiday.

*The tasty turkey has become a Thanksgiving symbol*

## THANKSGIVING TODAY

The modern American Thanksgiving is a mixture of old Pilgrim customs and new customs. Thanksgiving still has a serious, thoughtful side, like the Pilgrim Thanksgivings.

Modern Thanksgiving has also borrowed from the friendly, fun-loving spirit of the Pilgrims' Harvest Festival of 1621. Today, football games and family feasts are part of Thanksgiving celebrations.

*The roots of modern Thanksgivings are in the traditions of Pilgrims who arrived aboard the* Mayflower

## THE TURKEY AND THANKSGIVING

For most Americans, Thanksgiving would not be Thanksgiving without a turkey dinner. A Thanksgiving feast of turkey is an American tradition.

That tradition began with the Fall Harvest Festival of 1621. Wild turkey was probably not the only fowl served by the Pilgrims, but it may have been the tastiest. Turkey is certainly the Thanksgiving favorite today.

Most of the millions of turkeys served on Thanksgiving are raised on turkey farms.

## Glossary

**colonist** (KAH luh nihst) — someone who lives in a colony, especially someone who lived in England's colonies in America

**Congress** (KAHN gress) — in the United States, a group of lawmakers representing the states

**delegate** (DEL uh guht) — a person who represents a group; a person who is elected to speak or vote for many people

**national** (NAH shun ul) — of or relating to a nation

**recreation** (rek ree A shun) — fun and games

**tradition** (truh DISH un) — a group or family practice that has been carried on for many years; a custom